CHAPTER 1

TO BETTA FISH

Betta fish, scientifically known as Betta splendens, are captivating aquatic creatures that have found a special place in the hearts of aquarists around the world. Often referred to as Siamese fighting fish due to their occasional feistiness, Betta fish possess a remarkable combination of beauty and personality that sets them apart in the world of aquarium keeping.

Originating from Southeast Asia, particularly Thailand, Cambodia, Laos, and Vietnam, Betta fish have adapted to thrive in slow moving or stagnant waters like rice paddies, canals, and even roadside ditches. Understanding their natural habitat is key to providing optimal care in your home aquarium.

Betta fish come in a dazzling array of colors, fin shapes, and patterns. From the classic red, blue, and turquoise to the more exotic metallics, marbles, and dalmatians, the variety of colors and patterns is astonishing. Different fin types, such as veiltail, crowntail, and halfmoon, further contribute to the Betta's allure.

What makes Betta fish such a popular choice

for aquarists extends beyond their aesthetics. They possess unique personalities, with each Betta exhibiting distinct behaviors and quirks. Some Betta fish recognize their owners and interact with them, displaying curiosity, expressiveness, and occasionally even playfulness.

In this comprehensive guide, we'll delve deep into the world of Betta fish, unraveling the mysteries of their care, breeding, and the art of creating stunning Betta specific aquascapes. Betta fish keeping isn't just a hobby; it's a rewarding journey filled with discovery and wonder.

Prepare to embark on this voyage with us, and by the end of this guide, you'll be well equipped to master the art of Betta fish care, breeding, and aquascaping. Get ready to unlock the secrets of Betta fish mastery!

CHAPTER 2: SETTING UP THE

IDEAL BETTA HABITAT

Creating a comfortable and thriving environment for your Betta fish is paramount to their health and well being. In this chapter, we'll explore the essential aspects of setting up the perfect Betta habitat, ensuring your fish's happiness and longevity.

The foundation of an ideal Betta habitat begins with selecting the right aquarium. Although Betta fish are relatively small, they thrive when given ample space to swim and explore. A 5 gallon (or larger) aquarium is recommended for a single Betta, providing them with the freedom to display their natural behaviors and ensuring stable water conditions.

Maintaining stable water quality is crucial for the health of Betta fish. Fluctuations in water parameters can stress these fish and make them more susceptible to illnesses. Regular monitoring and regulation of parameters such as temperature, pH level, ammonia, nitrites, and nitrates are essential.

Temperature plays a pivotal role in the well being of Betta fish. Being tropical fish, they thrive in water with a stable temperature range of 78 F to 82 F (25.5 C 28 C). Utilizing a reliable aquarium heater is recommended to maintain the water temperature within this range.

Filtration and aeration are equally vital components of a Betta aquarium. Although Betta fish don't tolerate strong water currents, a gentle filter and aeration system are necessary for promoting oxygen exchange and eliminating impurities. Sponge filters and air stones are excellent choices for Betta tanks.

When it comes to decorating your Betta's habitat, you have the creative freedom to design an engaging and visually appealing environment. Betta fish enjoy having hiding spots, live or artificial plants, and substrate to explore. It's essential to select decorations and plants that are safe and non abrasive to avoid damaging your Betta's delicate fins.

In summary, creating the ideal Betta habitat involves careful planning and attention to detail. By choosing the right aquarium, maintaining stable water conditions, and providing suitable decor, you'll ensure that your Betta fish have a comfortable and thriving home.

CHAPTER 3: BETTA NUTRITION

AND FEEDING HABITS

A cornerstone of Betta fish care is providing them with proper nutrition. In this chapter, we'll dive deep into Betta nutrition and their feeding habits, ensuring that your fish receive the nutrients they need to thrive.

Understanding the dietary needs of Betta fish is the first step in providing them with the right nutrition. Betta fish are primarily carnivorous, which means their diet should consist of animal based protein. In their natural habitat, Betta fish feed on insects, larvae, and small aquatic creatures. To replicate this diet in captivity, consider offering them high quality Betta pellets or flakes with a high protein content.

Variety in their diet is key to providing optimal nutrition. Alongside pellets or flakes, you can offer freeze dried or frozen foods like bloodworms, daphnia, and brine shrimp. These foods provide essential nutrients and mirror the variety of prey they would encounter in the wild.

Establishing a feeding schedule is vital to prevent overfeeding and maintain water quality. Betta fish have small stomachs, and overfeeding can lead to health problems and water pollution. A general guideline is to feed your Betta fish small portions once or twice a day. Observe their behavior and adjust the feeding schedule based on their appetite. If they leave food uneaten, reduce the portion size in future feedings.

Occasional fasting days are beneficial for Betta fish. They can go without food for a day or two without harm, allowing their

digestive systems to rest and preventing digestive issues.

Always ensure that the food you provide is suitable for Betta fish. While they may show interest in other fish's food, not all fish food is appropriate for Bettas. Opt for food specifically formulated for Betta fish to meet their nutritional requirements.

By understanding Betta dietary needs and establishing a proper feeding routine, you'll contribute to your Betta's overall health and vitality.

CHAPTER 4: BETTA HEALTH

AND COMMON ISSUES

Recognizing signs of good health and being prepared to address common health issues are essential aspects of Betta fish care. In this chapter, we'll explore how to identify a healthy Betta, common health problems that Bettas may encounter, and effective strategies for prevention and treatment.

A healthy Betta fish exhibits several key traits:

Active swimming behavior

Vibrant and well maintained colors

Clear and undamaged fins and tail

No signs of distress or lethargy

Normal appetite and feeding behavior

Monitoring these characteristics regularly can help you detect any deviations from your Betta's usual behavior or appearance, which may indicate a health concern.

Despite their hardiness, Betta fish are susceptible to several common health issues, including:

Fin Rot: Recognizable by frayed or disintegrating fins and tail.

Ich (White Spot Disease): Characterized by white spots on the body and fins.

Fungus: Presents as cotton like growth on the skin or fins.

Constipation: Can cause bloating and difficulty swimming.

Preventing health issues begins with maintaining optimal water quality, as poor water conditions can stress Betta fish and make them more susceptible to illnesses. Regular water changes and water parameter monitoring are essential.

In the event that your Betta does develop a health issue, prompt treatment is crucial. Quarantine the affected fish to prevent the spread of disease, and consult a knowledgeable source or veterinarian for guidance on the most appropriate treatment.

This chapter aims to equip you with the knowledge and skills to keep your Betta fish in the best possible health. By understanding their basic needs, recognizing signs of illness, and knowing how to respond, you'll be well prepared to provide exceptional care for your Betta companions.

CHAPTER 5: BETTA BEHAVIOR

AND SOCIAL DYNAMICS

Betta fish are known for their unique behaviors and striking personalities. In this chapter, we'll delve into the fascinating world of Betta behavior, explore their social dynamics, and discover how to create a harmonious environment for your Betta companions.

Understanding Betta fish behavior is essential to ensure their well being. Bettas are highly territorial and can be aggressive toward other fish, especially males. This aggression is why they are often referred to as "Siamese fighting fish." It's crucial to provide each Betta with its separate living space to prevent conflicts and ensure their comfort.

Despite their territorial nature, Betta fish can still be quite interactive with their owners. They may recognize your presence and even follow your movements near the aquarium. Some Bettas even enjoy interacting with their owners by swimming near the glass or "dancing" in response to your finger movements. Building a bond with your Betta can be a rewarding aspect of Betta ownership.

When it comes to keeping multiple Bettas in one space, careful consideration is needed. While females can sometimes coexist in a larger tank with minimal issues, it's generally not recommended to house multiple males together unless you're experienced in managing their social dynamics.

Breeding behavior is another fascinating aspect of Betta behavior. Male Bettas perform elaborate courtship rituals to attract females, and these displays can be truly mesmerizing to witness. Breeding Betta fish can be a rewarding but challenging endeavor, and it's important to be well prepared and informed before attempting to breed them.

In this chapter, we'll also explore ways to provide mental stimulation for your Betta and enrich their environment. Bettas enjoy exploring their surroundings, so adding decorations, plants, and hiding spots can enhance their quality of life.

Overall, understanding Betta behavior and their social dynamics will help you create a harmonious and engaging environment for your Betta companions. By providing them with a safe and enriching habitat, you can enjoy the unique personalities and interactions that make Betta fish such captivating pets.

CHAPTER 6: BREEDING BETTA FISH

Breeding Betta fish is a fascinating and rewarding endeavor for aquarists who are ready to take their Betta mastery to the next level. In this chapter, we'll explore the intricate world of Betta breeding, from preparing for the breeding process to rearing and caring for Betta fry.

Preparing for Betta Breeding

Before embarking on the breeding journey, it's essential to be well prepared. Breeding Betta fish requires careful planning and attention to detail. Here are the steps to prepare for Betta breeding:

Selecting Breeding Pairs: Choose healthy and mature Betta fish for breeding. Ensure that the male and female are in prime condition and exhibit vibrant colors and good fin development.

Conditioning: Properly condition the breeding pair by feeding them a nutritious and varied diet. Live or frozen foods can be especially beneficial during this period.

Breeding Tank Setup: Prepare a separate breeding tank, ideally with a capacity of 10 20 gallons. Include plenty of hiding spots for the female to seek refuge from the male's advances.

Temperature and Water Quality: Maintain stable water conditions with a temperature around 80 82 F (27 28 C). Keep water parameters pristine, as clean water is essential for successful breeding.

Introduction: Place the male and female in separate compartments within the breeding tank to allow them to see each other without direct contact. Observe their behavior and readiness for breeding.

The Breeding Process Unveiled

Betta breeding involves a series of complex behaviors and courtship rituals. When the male and female are ready, introduce them into the breeding tank and closely monitor

their interactions. The male will build a
bubble nest at the water's surface, and
the female will contribute by releasing her
eggs. The male will then fertilize the eggs,
and the female should be removed to prevent
aggression.

Rearing and Caring for Betta Fry

After successful fertilization, the male Betta
will care for the eggs and, later, the fry.
This paternal care includes tending to the
bubble nest, guarding the fry, and ensuring
they receive adequate oxygen from the nest. As
the fry hatch and become free swimming, it's
crucial to provide them with proper nutrition,
such as infusoria and later, newly hatched

brine shrimp.

Breeding Betta fish can be a challenging but incredibly rewarding experience. It allows you to witness the full life cycle of these remarkable fish and create a new generation of Bettas with unique characteristics. As you venture into the world of Betta breeding, remember that patience and attention to detail are key to success.

CHAPTER 7: CREATING STUNNING

BETTA AQUASCAPES

One of the joys of Betta fish keeping is the opportunity to create stunning aquascapes that not only showcase your Bettas but also provide them with an enriched environment. In this chapter, we'll explore the aesthetic appeal of Betta specific aquascapes and provide insights into creating captivating underwater landscapes.

The Aesthetic Appeal of Betta Specific Aquascapes

Betta fish are natural focal points in any aquarium due to their vibrant colors and graceful fins. Designing a Betta specific aquascape allows you to complement their beauty and create a visually striking display. Here are some key aspects to consider:

- Plant Selection and Placement: Choose live or artificial plants that are Betta friendly. Bettas appreciate resting spots near the water's surface, so floating plants like Amazon Frogbit or Water Lettuce can be excellent additions.

- Hardscape Design Ideas: Incorporate driftwood, rocks, or other hardscape elements to create a visually appealing layout. Avoid sharp or abrasive decorations that could harm your Betta's delicate fins.

- Lighting Considerations: Proper lighting can enhance the colors of both your Betta fish and the aquatic plants. Opt for adjustable LED lights that allow you to customize the intensity and color spectrum to showcase your Betta's beauty.

- Maintenance for Aquascapes: Regular maintenance is essential to keep your Betta aquascape thriving. Prune and trim plants as needed, clean the substrate, and perform water changes to maintain optimal water quality.

Creating a stunning Betta aquascape not only enhances the aesthetics of your aquarium but also provides enrichment for your Betta fish. They can explore and interact with the plants and decor, making their environment more engaging.

As you design and maintain your Betta aquascape, remember that it's a dynamic and evolving art form. You can continuously refine and adapt your aquascape to suit your Betta's preferences and your artistic vision.

CHAPTER 8: BETTA REPRODUCTION:

FROM COURTSHIP TO FRY CARE

Reproduction is a significant aspect of Betta fish's life cycle, and understanding the intricacies of this process is crucial for responsible Betta ownership. In this chapter, we'll take an in depth look at Betta reproduction, from courtship rituals to fry care.

The Courtship Rituals of Betta Fish

Betta courtship is a mesmerizing display of color, fin flare, and dance like movements. Male Bettas are the initiators, showcasing their vibrant colors and unique fin types to attract females. The courtship process typically unfolds in the following stages:

The Male's Invitation: The male begins by building a bubble nest at the water's surface. This nest consists of tiny bubbles held together by a secretion from the male's mouth.

Female's Interest: When a female Betta enters the male's territory, he intensifies his courtship efforts, displaying vibrant colors and flaring his fins. The female may show her interest by approaching the male and responding to his advances.

The Spawning Act: The male initiates the actual spawning act by wrapping his body around the female, prompting her to release her eggs. Simultaneously, the male fertilizes the eggs externally.

Bubble Nest Care: After fertilization, the male carefully gathers the eggs and places them in his bubble nest. He guards the nest diligently, ensuring the eggs remain safe and well aerated.

Rearing Betta Fry

Once the eggs hatch, the male continues to care for the fry, guarding them and providing protection. Initially, the fry rely on their yolk sacs for nutrition, but as they grow, they transition to more substantial food sources.

Feeding Betta fry can be a delicate process. Infusoria, tiny microorganisms, and later, newly hatched brine shrimp or specialized fry food, are suitable choices. Frequent and small feedings are essential, as overfeeding can lead to water quality issues.

Separating the Fry

After a few weeks, it's advisable to separate the fry from the male Betta to prevent any potential aggression or accidental predation. Transfer the fry to a separate grow out tank equipped with appropriate filtration and heating.

CHAPTER 9: ADVANCED BETTA

CARE TECHNIQUES

Once you've mastered the basics of Betta fish keeping, you may want to explore advanced care techniques to further enhance the well being of your Betta companions. In this chapter, we'll delve into advanced Betta care strategies, from tailored nutrition to breeding challenges.

Customized Betta Nutrition

As you become more experienced in Betta care, you may want to experiment with customizing your Betta's diet to enhance their health and vibrancy. While high quality Betta pellets and flakes form the foundation of their diet, you can supplement their meals with a variety of live and frozen foods.

Selective Breeding

For those interested in breeding Bettas, selective breeding allows you to develop unique color patterns, fin types, and other desirable traits. This advanced technique involves carefully choosing breeding pairs based on specific genetic characteristics.

Aquascaping Masterclass

Elevate your Betta's aquatic environment by delving deeper into the art of aquascaping. Advanced aquascaping involves more intricate layouts, precise plant choices, and a meticulous approach to detail.

Health and Disease Management

Advanced Betta enthusiasts are well versed in identifying and treating various health issues. By building your knowledge of Betta diseases and their treatments, you can provide swift and effective care when needed.

Community Tank Considerations

For those looking to create a community tank with Betta fish, understanding compatible tankmates, and managing social dynamics becomes crucial. You'll explore the art of community tank setups and maintain harmony among different species.

This chapter aims to provide you with

insights into advanced Betta care techniques, allowing you to take your Betta fish keeping to new heights. Whether you're interested in breeding, aquascaping, or specialized nutrition, these advanced strategies will help you provide exceptional care for your Betta companions.

CHAPTER 10: CONCLUSION

As you reach the conclusion of this comprehensive guide, you've embarked on a remarkable journey into the world of Betta fish. You've gained insights into their care, behavior, breeding, and the art of creating stunning aquascapes. You've learned to recognize signs of good health and address common issues, ensuring your Betta companions thrive.

Remember that Betta fish keeping is not just a hobby; it's a rewarding and fulfilling endeavor. The bond you form with your Betta companions, the beauty of their aquatic world, and the knowledge you've acquired are all part of this extraordinary experience.

Whether you're a beginner taking your first steps or an experienced Betta enthusiast seeking advanced techniques, the world of Betta fish offers endless opportunities for exploration and discovery. Your Betta companions will continue to amaze you with their unique personalities and captivating behaviors.

Thank you for joining us on this journey of Betta fish mastery. May your Betta fish thrive, your aquascapes dazzle, and your passion for these remarkable creatures continue to grow.

Made in United States
Troutdale, OR
12/12/2023

15786149R00022